The
OCTOBER CRISIS

Weigl

Published by Weigl Educational Publishers Limited
6325 10th Street S.E.
Calgary, AB T2H 2Z9
Website: www.weigl.com

Library and Archives Canada Cataloguing-in-Publication Data available upon request.
Fax (403) 233-7769 for the attention of the Publishing Records department.

ISBN 978-1-77071-613-1

Printed in the United States of America in North Mankato, Minnesota
1 2 3 4 5 6 7 8 9 0 14 13 12 11 10

072010
WEP230610

Project Coordinator: Heather C. Hudak
Author: Penny Dowdy
Editor: Bill Becker

We gratefully acknowledge the financial support of the Government of Canada
through the Canada Book Fund for our publishing activities.

Contents

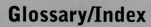

Overview

During the 1960s, the province of Quebec experienced a push for modernization. The French-Canadian province improved its school system, limited the influence of the Catholic Church in government, and pushed for improved working conditions. This modernization also caused many people to call for an independent nation.

One group that called for an independent Quebec was the *Front de Libération du Quebec*, or FLQ. The FLQ used violence and **scare tactics** to push for independence. In October 1970, the FLQ kidnapped a British **diplomat** and a Canadian government official. The government reacted by enacting the **War Measures Act** and limiting the rights of people they thought were associated with the FLQ. The crisis, called the October Crisis or the FLQ Crisis, ended with one victim murdered and a second victim safely released.

Background Information

James Cross - James Cross was a British trade commissioner who was kidnapped by the FLQ, sparking the October Crisis.

Pierre Laporte - Pierre Laporte was the Quebec labour minister who was kidnapped by the same terrorist group shortly after James Cross was kidnapped.

Pierre Trudeau - Canadian Prime Minister Pierre Trudeau helped put an end to the October Crisis.

Robert Bourassa - Robert Bourassa was the premier of Quebec when the FLQ kidnapped Cross and Laporte.

Marc Carbonneau - Marc Carbonneau was one of the political activists responsible for the kidnapping of James Cross.

Paul Rose - Paul Rose was a political activist who helped kidnap Pierre Laporte.

THE FRENCH AND BRITISH COMPETED FOR LAND AND MONEY IN CANADA THROUGHOUT THE 1700S.

I CAN GET YOU THE BEST QUALITY SKINS IN THE AREA.

THAT TRADER WILL CHARGE YOU FAR MORE THAN THOSE SKINS ARE WORTH! MY SKINS COME AT A FAIR PRICE.

THE BRITISH, FRENCH, AND ABORIGINAL PEOPLES FOUGHT FOR CONTROL OF TRADE AND LAND IN THE SEVEN YEARS' WAR. WHEN THE WAR ENDED, GREAT BRITAIN GAINED CONTROL OF FRENCH CANADA.

WE CLAIM THIS TERRITORY FOR THE CROWN OF GREAT BRITAIN!

GREAT BRITAIN MAY CONTROL THE LAND, BUT I WILL ALWAYS HAVE FRANCE IN MY SOUL.

THOUGH CANADA REMAINED UNDER BRITISH CONTROL UNTIL IT BECAME AN INDEPENDENT NATION, FRENCH-CANADIAN CULTURE HAS ALWAYS BEEN A STRONG PART OF THE CANADIAN IDENTITY.

O CANADA! OUR HOME AND NATIVE LAND!

O CANADA! TERRE DE NOS AÏEUX!

SEPARATIST GROUPS BEGAN TO CALL FOR A SOVEREIGN QUEBEC.

INDEPENDENCE FOR QUEBEC!

VIVE LE QUÉBEC LIBRE! LONG LIVE FREE QUEBEC!

ONE OF THESE SEPARATIST GROUPS WAS THE *FRONT DE LIBÉRATION DU QUEBEC*, OR THE FLQ. STARTING IN 1963, THE FLQ BEGAN PREPARING TO USE **TERRORISM** TO GAIN QUEBEC'S INDEPENDENCE. SOME OF THE TERRORISTS WENT TO CUBA TO LEARN **GUERRILLA WARFARE**.

THIS IS THE ONLY WAY THE PEOPLE OF QUEBEC WILL RISE UP AND FREE THEMSELVES OF CANADIAN RULE.

11

DURING WORLD WAR I, SOME PEOPLE LIVING IN CANADA WERE FROM THE COUNTRIES THAT CANADIAN TROOPS WERE FIGHTING, SUCH AS AUSTRIA-HUNGARY. THE WAR MEASURES ACT LIMITED WHAT THESE IMMIGRANTS COULD DO WHILE LIVING IN CANADA. FOR EXAMPLE, PEOPLE FROM COUNTRIES THAT SUPPORTED AUSTRIA-HUNGARY HAD TO CARRY IDENTIFICATION PAPERS. THEY COULD NOT OWN GUNS. SOME WERE FORCED OUT OF THE COUNTRY.

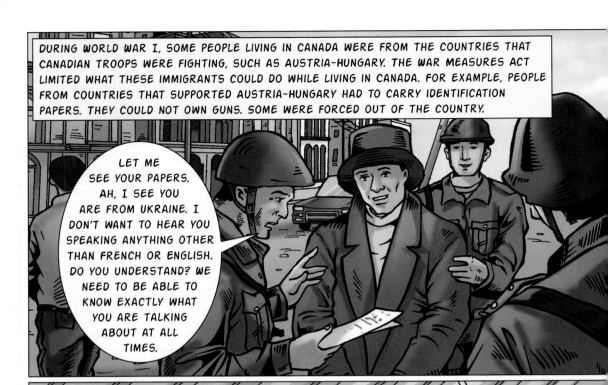

LET ME SEE YOUR PAPERS. AH, I SEE YOU ARE FROM UKRAINE. I DON'T WANT TO HEAR YOU SPEAKING ANYTHING OTHER THAN FRENCH OR ENGLISH. DO YOU UNDERSTAND? WE NEED TO BE ABLE TO KNOW EXACTLY WHAT YOU ARE TALKING ABOUT AT ALL TIMES.

IN WORLD WAR II, CANADA WAS AT WAR WITH JAPAN. AGAIN, THE GOVERNMENT ENFORCED THE WAR MEASURES ACT. ANY PEOPLE LIVING IN CANADA WHO WERE OF JAPANESE DESCENT WERE HELD IN **INTERNMENT CAMPS**, AND THE GOVERNMENT TOOK THEIR MONEY AND PROPERTY.

I DON'T UNDERSTAND WHY THEY ARE KEEPING US HERE. I WAS BORN IN CANADA. MY PARENTS MOVED HERE BEFORE I WAS EVEN BORN.

I OWNED A SUCCESSFUL BUSINESS. THEY TOOK EVERYTHING AWAY FROM ME. MY FAMILY HAS NO HOME. WE'VE DONE NOTHING WRONG.

THE FLQ CRISIS WAS THE FIRST TIME THE GOVERNMENT USED THE WMA WHEN CANADA WAS NOT AT WAR. THE WMA ALLOWED THE MILITARY TO LOOK FOR PEOPLE WHO MIGHT BE WORKING WITH THE FLQ OR SUPPORTING QUEBEC'S INDEPENDENCE.

WHY ARE YOU SEARCHING MY HOME? YOU HAVE NO PROOF THAT I HAVE COMMITTED ANY CRIME.

BY SUNRISE THE MORNING AFTER THE WMA WAS ENACTED, CANADIAN OFFICIALS HAD ARRESTED MORE THAN 240 PEOPLE.

WHAT DO YOU KNOW ABOUT THE FLQ? WHERE DO THEY HAVE CROSS AND LAPORTE?

I DON'T KNOW ANYTHING ABOUT THE FLQ! I HAVE NOTHING TO DO WITH THEM! PLEASE, LET ME GO HOME.

THE USE OF THE WMA TO MAKE ARRESTS ANGERED THE FLQ. THEY SENT WORD ON OCTOBER 17TH TO LEADERS IN QUEBEC THAT LAPORTE WOULD BE KILLED. HIS BODY WAS FOUND THAT EVENING IN THE TRUNK OF A CAR. HE HAD BEEN STRANGLED.

"FACED WITH THE ARROGANCE OF THE FEDERAL GOVERNMENT AND OF ITS VALET BOURASSA, FACED WITH THEIR OBVIOUS BAD FAITH, THE FLQ HAS DECIDED TO ACT..."

WHEN WORD OF LAPORTE'S MURDER WAS RELEASED, PEOPLE GATHERED TO EXPRESS THEIR SADNESS. AT THE SAME TIME, HUNDREDS MORE PEOPLE WERE ARRESTED UNDER SUSPICION OF SUPPORTING THE FLQ.

SECURITY WAS VERY HIGH AT LAPORTE'S FUNERAL. IF THE FLQ WANTED TO LAUNCH ANOTHER ATTACK, MANY OF CANADA'S LEADERS WOULD BE THERE. SOLDIERS KEPT WATCH FOR ANYTHING OR ANYONE SUSPICIOUS.

I'M SO SORRY FOR YOUR LOSS, MRS. LAPORTE.

THE CANADIAN GOVERNMENT HELD PRISONERS WITHOUT CHARGES THAT WERE SUSPECTED OF WORKING WITH THE FLQ. THE ARMY DID NOT HAVE TO ALLOW THE PRISONERS TO SEE LAWYERS, FAMILY, OR FRIENDS. MANY CANADIANS WERE VERY ANGRY OVER THE ARRESTS. OTHERS WERE UNCOMFORTABLE WITH ARMY OFFICERS PATROLLING AND SEARCHING.

CAN I SPEAK TO MY LAWYER? MY FAMILY? I'VE BEEN HERE FOR 10 DAYS ALREADY!

NO LAWYERS. NO FAMILY. YOU WILL HAVE NO CONTACT WITH PEOPLE OUTSIDE THIS JAIL.

A NUMBER OF CITIZENS FELT THAT THE WMA WAS THE WRONG APPROACH TO FIXING THE PROBLEMS IN QUEBEC.

IF THE GOVERNMENT TOOK BETTER CARE OF THE PEOPLE OF QUEBEC, THE FLQ WOULD NOT HAVE TURNED VIOLENT. THE GOVERNMENT SHOULD MAKE SURE THAT FRENCH CANADIANS ARE PAID A FAIR AMOUNT, THAT THEIR HOMES ARE SAFE, AND THEY HAVE THE SAME OPPORTUNITIES AS ENGLISH-SPEAKING CITIZENS.

THE REVOLUTION THAT THE FLQ HOPED TO START DID NOT HAPPEN. ALTHOUGH PEOPLE INSISTED ON CHANGES IN QUEBEC, THE CALLS FOR INDEPENDENCE DID NOT INCREASE. THE FLQ HOPED THAT COLLEGE STUDENTS AND PROFESSORS WOULD RALLY BEHIND THE CAUSE OF A SOVEREIGN QUEBEC. THIS DID NOT HAPPEN.

WHAT HAPPENED TO THE STUDENTS WHO WERE SUPPORTING THE FLQ?

THEY PROBABLY MOVED ON TO ANOTHER CAUSE. I HAVEN'T HEARD ANYONE TALK ABOUT SOVEREIGNTY IN WEEKS.

BY NOVEMBER, 439 PEOPLE HAD BEEN ARRESTED, AND ALL BUT 60 HAD BEEN RELEASED.

WE WERE SO WORRIED! ARE YOU OKAY?

I AM NOW. THANK GOODNESS THIS ORDEAL IS FINALLY OVER.

THE POLICE AND ARMY CONTINUED TO LOOK FOR CROSS AND HIS KIDNAPPERS. ON DECEMBER 3, 1970, THEY LOCATED THE HOUSE WHERE CROSS HAD BEEN HELD.

WE KNOW YOU'RE IN THERE! RELEASE MR. CROSS IMMEDIATELY!

MARC CARBONNEAU AND THE OTHER KIDNAPPERS AGREED TO SET CROSS FREE IF THE POLICE LET THEM ESCAPE.

WHAT DO YOU NEED?

WE WANT A CAR TO THE AIRPORT AND A PLANE READY TO TAKE US TO CUBA.

WE CAN DO THAT, BUT WE WANT CROSS UNHARMED.

THE FLQ HANDED CROSS OVER TO AUTHORITIES, AND THE KIDNAPPERS ESCAPED TO CUBA UNHARMED.

WE CAN SEE CROSS IN THE CAR WITH THE FLQ KIDNAPPERS. HE IS ALIVE AND WELL. THE KIDNAPPERS WILL RELEASE HIM ONCE THEY ARRIVE AT THEIR PLANE.

NEWS

AIRPORT

CARBONNEAU STAYED IN CUBA UNTIL 1973, WHEN HE SECRETLY LEFT TO LIVE IN FRANCE. HE WANTED TO RETURN TO CANADA, SO HE NEGOTIATED HIS SURRENDER IN 1982.

MARC CARBONNEAU, YOU ARE UNDER ARREST FOR THE KIDNAPPING OF JAMES CROSS.

PAUL ROSE WAS ARRESTED FOR THE KIDNAPPING AND MURDER OF PIERRE LAPORTE. HE WAS SENTENCED TO LIFE IN PRISON. LATER, EVIDENCE SHOWED THAT HE WAS NOT INVOLVED IN LAPORTE'S MURDER, AND HE WAS RELEASED FROM PRISON IN 1982.

HOW DO I PROVE I DIDN'T KILL THE MAN I KIDNAPPED?

ROBERT BOURASSA WAS RE-ELECTED AS PREMIER OF QUEBEC IN 1973. HE RAN AGAIN IN 1985 AND SERVED UNTIL 1994. BOURASSA'S DECISION TO SEEK FEDERAL HELP DURING THE FLQ CRISIS DID NOT HURT HIS POLITICAL CAREER.

I AM HONOURED TO SERVE YOU AGAIN AS PREMIER OF QUEBEC.

PIERRE TRUDEAU SERVED AS PRIME MINISTER UNTIL 1984. HE HELPED STRENGTHEN THE UNITY OF THE COUNTRY AND FELT THAT ALL CULTURES HAD A PLACE IN CANADA.

"I BELIEVE A CONSTITUTION CAN PERMIT THE CO-EXISTENCE OF SEVERAL CULTURES AND ETHNIC GROUPS WITHIN A SINGLE STATE."

A SMALL NUMBER OF ROYAL CANADIAN MOUNTED POLICE WERE CHARGED WITH BREAKING THE LAW DURING THE OCTOBER CRISIS.

THE NOTES FROM THE FLQ THAT YOU SHOWED US WERE FAKE. DID YOU WRITE THEM YOURSELF?

YES SIR, I DID.

YOUR BEHAVIOUR IS A BLACK MARK ON THE REPUTATION OF THE ROYAL CANADIAN MOUNTED POLICE. YOU'RE FIRED.

IN 1988, PARLIAMENT PASSED THE EMERGENCIES ACT TO DEAL WITH EMERGENCY SITUATIONS DURING PEACE TIME. THE EMERGENCIES ACT IS MORE SPECIFIC AS TO WHAT ACTIONS CAN BE TAKEN IN A **NATIONAL EMERGENCY**, AND IT DOES NOT CURTAIL THE CIVIL RIGHTS OF CITIZENS THE WAY THE WMA DID. THE WMA WAS REPEALED.

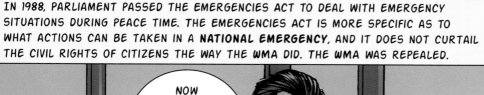

NOW WE CAN REVOKE THE EMERGENCY POWERS IF THEY ARE MISUSED.

YES, AND CANADIAN CITIZENS CAN KEEP THEIR **FUNDAMENTAL** CIVIL RIGHTS, EVEN IN A NATIONAL EMERGENCY.

Brain Teasers

1. How did French culture become so rich in parts of Canada?

2. What happened during the Quiet Revolution?

3. What did separatists want during the October Crisis?

4. What made the FLQ different from other separatist groups?

5. What did the police do in order to secure James Cross's release?

6. How did the FLQ terrorize the people of Quebec?

7. Why did some officials in Quebec oppose calling
   Prime Minister Trudeau?

1. The French had settlements starting at the St. Lawrence River hundreds of years ago.
2. The province of Quebec gained more control over health care and education, and changes to labour policies gave French Canadians an opportunity to earn wages comparable to those earned by English Canadians.
3. Separatists wanted Quebec to become independent of Canada.
4. The FLQ used terrorism to try to gain independence for Quebec.
5. They negotiated with the FLQ and allowed the kidnappers to escape to Cuba.
6. The FLQ stole weapons, set off bombs, kidnapped government officials, and killed Pierre Laporte.
7. The officials felt that the problem was a local one, rather than a problem that needed the federal government's involvement.

Further Information

How can I find out more about the October Crisis?

Most libraries have computers that connect to a database that contains information on books and articles about different subjects. You can input a key word and find material on the person, place, or thing you want to learn more about. The computer will provide you with a list of books in the library that contain information on the subject you searched for. Non-fiction books are arranged numerically, using their call number. Fiction books are organized alphabetically by the author's last name.

Books

Craats, Rennay. *The 1970s*. Calgary: Weigl Educational Publishers Limited, 2000.

Tetley, William. *The October Crisis, 1970: An Insider's View*. Montreal: McGill-Queen's University Press, 2007.

Trudeau, Pierre Elliott. *Memoirs*. Toronto, Ont.: McClelland & Stewart, 1993.

Websites

http://archives.cbc.ca/politics/civil_unrest/topics/101
Archived reports from the Canadian Broadcasting Corporation reporting on the FLQ Crisis

www.histori.ca/peace/page.do?pageID=342
Historica-Dominion Institute's website, providing text and images describing the FLQ Crisis

Glossary

civil rights: freedoms all individuals have that are guaranteed by the Constitution

committed: performed

diplomat: a government representative

economic: related to making, selling, and buying goods and services

federal government: the central law-making body of a country or nation

fundamental: basic; of central importance

guerrilla warfare: military action using small mobile forces to carry out surprise attacks

internment camps: prison camps for people of foreign descent, prisoners of war, or political prisoners

national emergency: a crisis that impacts an entire country or nation

scare tactics: using acts that cause fear to influence a reaction

separatist: a person who wants to be apart from a group

sovereign: supreme authority over a state or nation

terrorism: using scare tactics or violence to achieve a goal

War Measures Act: a federal law that allowed the Canadian government to assume sweeping emergency powers

Index